A captivating pastel sunrise over the Bourgeau Range promises a lovely day.

Publication Information

Copyright 1996 © Altitude Publishing Canada Ltd.
Text © 1996 Alec Pytlowany

Canadian Cataloguing in Publication Data
Pytlowany, Alec, 1955–
Winter in the Canadian Rockies

ISBN 1-55153-114-3 (hd) -- ISBN 1-55153-115-1 (pb)
1. Rocky Mountains, Canadian (B.C. and Alta.)--Pictorial
works.* 2. Winter--Rocky Mountains, Canadian (B.C. and
Alta.)--Pictorial works.* 3. Rocky Mountains, Canadian (B.C.
and Alta.)--Description.* 4. Winter--Rocky Mountains,
Canadian (B.C. and Alta.)* I. Title.
FC219.P97 1996   971.1'04'0222   C96-910461-8
F1090.P97 1996

Altitude GreenTree Program
Altitude will plant, in Canada, twice as many trees as were used
in the manufacturing of this book.

Made in Western Canada
Printed and bound in Canada
by Friesen Printers, Altona, Manitoba

Design	Stephen Hutchings
Text	Alec Pytlowany
Editor	Jill Dominique
Electronic page layout	Sandra Davis and Sharon Komori
Financial management	Laurie Smith

Photographic credits
All photos are by Alec Pytlowany
except: Dennis Schmidt: page 26 (middle left)
Esther Schmidt: page 26 (top), page 27 (top and middle right)

Altitude Publishing Canada Ltd.
1500 Railway Avenue, Canmore, Alberta, T0L 0M0

WINTER IN THE CANADIAN ROCKIES

Late afternoon light on the Fairholme Range is reflected in Vermilion Lake.

Contents

WINTER IN THE ROCKIES

Winter winds sweep snow across the face of Mt. Temple.

To visit Banff and Lake Louise in winter is to be captivated by the spectacular natural beauty of a pristine alpine wilderness and embraced by the rich heritage of genuine western Canadian hospitality. It is a vacation experience unlike any other: three outstanding alpine ski resorts draped in fluffy, dry powder snow, an endless variety of recreational activities and attractions, a variety of wilderness adventures, and two charming mountain communities teeming with aprés–ski excitement, unique culture, and uncompromising comfort and service.

Surrounded by the immense wilderness and wildlife preserve of Banff National Park, the resort destinations of Banff and Lake Louise offer an experience that is becoming increasingly rare. In 1985, the United Nations designated the special lands of Banff National Park as a World Heritage Site.

This book, which showcases the extraordinary talents of Banff photographer Alec Pytlowany, celebrates the uncommon pride that park residents share for the precious lands they inhabit and their lasting commitment to the promise that future generations will enjoy unimpaired wilderness. These pages embrace the breathtaking winter scenery of Banff and Lake Louise and invite the reader to visit a special place–a place we call home.

Opposite: Majestic Mount Assiniboine is fittingly known as the "Matterhorn of the Canadian Rockies."

Top: For world travellers, Banff and Lake Louise are the most recognizable destinations in the Canadian Rockies. But just 30 kilometres from the Banff townsite, near the border of Banff National Park, sits the charming town of Canmore. One of Canmore's more prominent peaks, the Three Sisters, rises behind the townsite.

Once a coal-mining town, Canmore now thrives as a tourist destination, as well as a service centre for the 17,000 residents of the Bow Valley.

Bottom: The Canmore Nordic Centre, originally built to host the cross-country skiing events of the 1988 Winter Olympics, remains a very popular Olympic legacy enjoyed by residents and visitors alike. Here we see the opening ceremonies for an international cross-country skiing competition.

Top: The Fairholme Range provides a backdrop for one of Banff's three Vermilion Lakes. Connected by marshes and beaver dams, the three lakes are a significant wetlands for migratory birds. Wildlife such as elk, deer, muskrat, and the occasional moose and wolf, can be seen visiting lakes during the winter months.

Overleaf: Dusk settles over statuesque Mount Rundle and the Bow Valley. The mountain was named for the Reverend Robert Rundle, a Methodist missionary to the Plains Indians who visited Banff in 1847.

Bottom: Musher James Tribe moves his dogsled team through rugged mountain terrain. Companies in Lake Louise, Banff and Canmore provide guided dogsled tours. Canmore Nordic Centre is the site each winter for an exciting international dogsled competition.

BANFF

Moonlight glows on Cascade Mountain while the lights of a winter's night illuminate Banff Avenue.

For over 100 years, Banff has played a prominent role in the life of Canada. Following the discovery of hot mineral springs at the site of the Cave and Basin in 1885, the Canadian Pacific Railway (CPR) built a major hotel–the Banff Springs–at the top of the Bow Falls near the Upper Hot Springs on Sulphur Mountain. This hotel became the focus for a full-scale marketing campaign, over a century ago, launched by the CPR to promote their hotels and their inter-continental railway system.

The town of Banff grew quickly to help service the railway and its imposing hotel. However, it was not long before the town be-came famous in its own right as a centre of civilization nestled in the heart of a vast alpine wilderness.

The long winters in Banff were the perfect time to pursue winter sports such as cross-country skiing, snowshoeing, dog sledding and ice skating. Today, three world-class snow-boarding and downhill ski areas add to this list and attract thousands of people who are look-ing for a perfect winter vacation.

Winter nights in Banff are just as warm and merry as they were 100 years ago: dining over sumptuous meals, dancing, socializing, or just sitting in front of a roaring log fire embracing breathtaking winter scenery.

Opposite: Cascade Mountain looms above Banff Avenue.

Top: With the greens covered in snow and the carts temporarily stored away, the Banff Springs Hotel Golf Course becomes a mecca for cross-country skiers during the winter months.

Overleaf: The full perspective of Banff townsite and its surrounding topography can be obtained from the observation deck on Sulphur Mountain. (inset) The same view at night shows the limits of civilization.

Opposite: Goat Mountain dwarfs the 846-room Banff Springs Hotel.

Bottom: The Banff Springs Hotel is known as "The Castle in the Rockies." This night view illustrates why.

Cascade Mountain and the town of Banff

1. Cascade Mtn.
2. Mt. Norquay
3. Stoney Squaw Mtn.
4. Highway #1
5. Vermilion Lakes
6. Bow River
7. Town of Banff
8. Bow Falls
9. Banff Springs Hotel
10. Banff Springs Hotel Golf Course
11. The Banff Centre
12. Tunnel Mtn.
13. Mt. Aylmer
14. Lake Minnewanka
15. Johnson Lake
16. Bankhead

to Sunshine and Lake Louise

to Canmore
and Calgary

Top: Cascade Mountain overlooks Banff Avenue, the town's centre of activity. Restaurants, retail shops and attractions draw millions of visitors to this engaging alpine village. Banff has restored and maintained many of its heritage buildings, ensuring that future generations can appreciate the town's historical significance.

Opposite: Dawn brings an orange glow to Cascade Mountain. First ascended in 1887, its ice falls remain a challenge for today's climbers.

Bottom: Mount Inglismaldie provides the backdrop for the historic Banff train station which services international freight year-round and touring passengers during the summer.

Top: A skilled ice carver finishes his team's glistening entry in "Ice Magic," the International Ice Carving Competition which is held each January in Lake Louise.
Bottom left: Music, theatre and dance, can be enjoyed at the Eric Harvey Theatre at the Banff Centre throughout the year. This is a scene from the classic ballet, the *Nutcracker.*
Bottom right: The Banff Arts Festival brings a rich cultural agenda to Banff.
Opposite top: The rugged Sawback Range reflects its finest dusk colours in an orange alpen-glow.
Opposite bottom: A dramatic torchlight parade of skiers snakes down the slopes of Mount Norquay as part of a New Year's celebration.

Top: First opened in 1993, The Banff Caribou Lodge is a good example of the contemporary alpine architecture typical of Banff's newer buildings. Visitors will find a wide selection of accommodations from which to choose, including premium-and moderately-priced hotels, motor inns, bed and breakfasts, hostels, and winter camping facilities.

Opposite: Bells peal from the snow-dusted spires of the lovely Presbyterian Church on Banff Avenue at Wolf Street.

Overleaf: The beautiful Bow Falls, pictured here with Mt. Brewster in the background, are part of the Bow River, which flows year round.

The Bow begins its journey 90 km northwest of the town of Banff, at Bow Glacier, part of the Wapta Icefields. After it leaves Banff, the Bow flows east through Canmore to Calgary. This river provides some of the world's best trout fishing.

Bottom: The dining opportuni- ties in Banff are diverse and delectable.

Top: The lights of Banff townsite glow beneath the peak of Mt. Rundle. This view is from the Mount Norquay road.

Bottom: Banff offers a diverse assortment of activities and experiences—all in close proximity to the town.

Opposite top: Framed by snow- sheathed lodgepole pine, Mount Brewster looms above the valley fog. Mt. Brewster is one of the steeply tilted limestone mountains of the Front Range, an area encompassing 2,000 square kilometres of wilderness.

Opposite bottom: Banff's renowned mineral springs are available to bathers year-round at the Upper Hot Springs pool, where water temperatures average 47.3 degrees C. A new spa featuring a steam room and plunge opened in 1996.

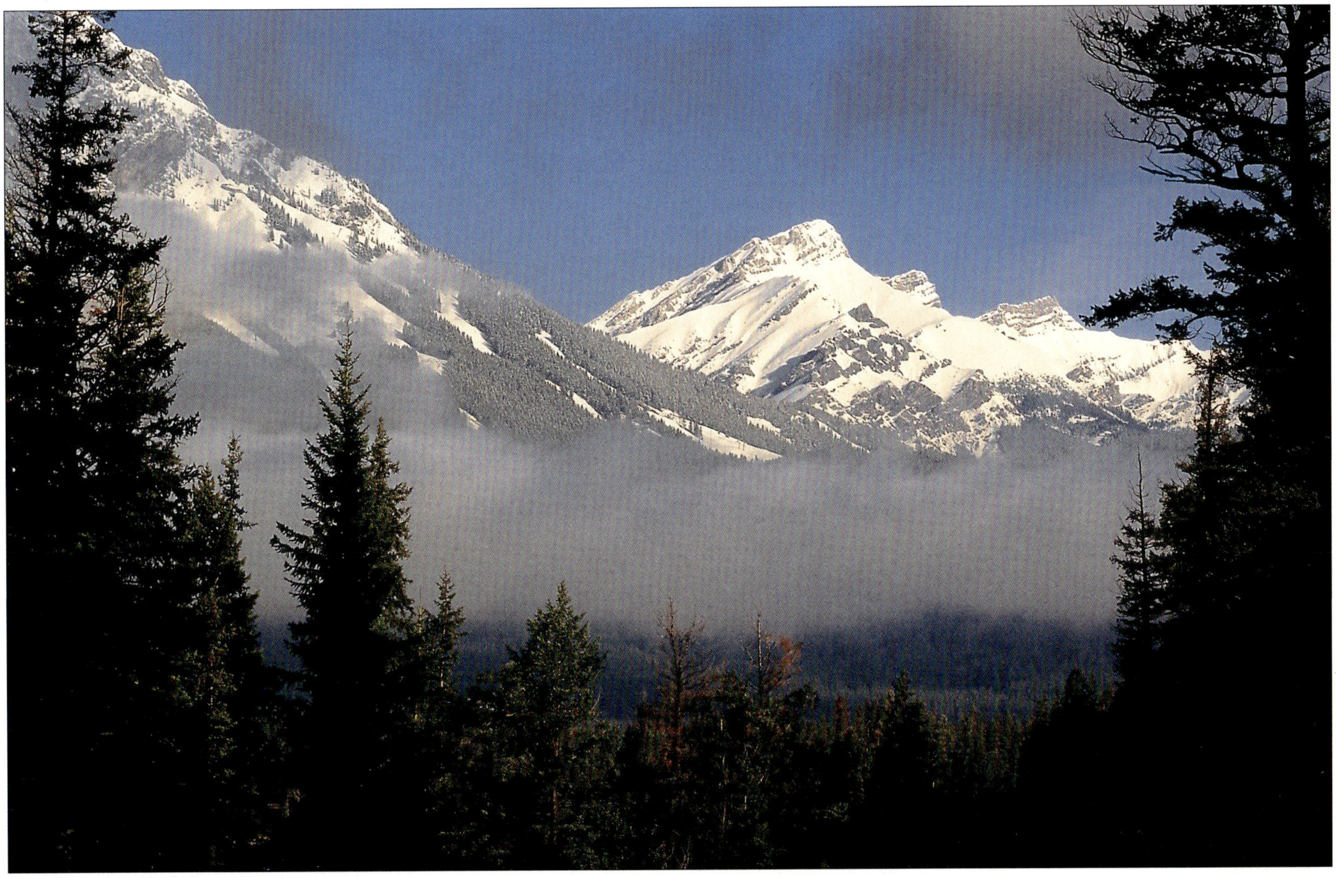

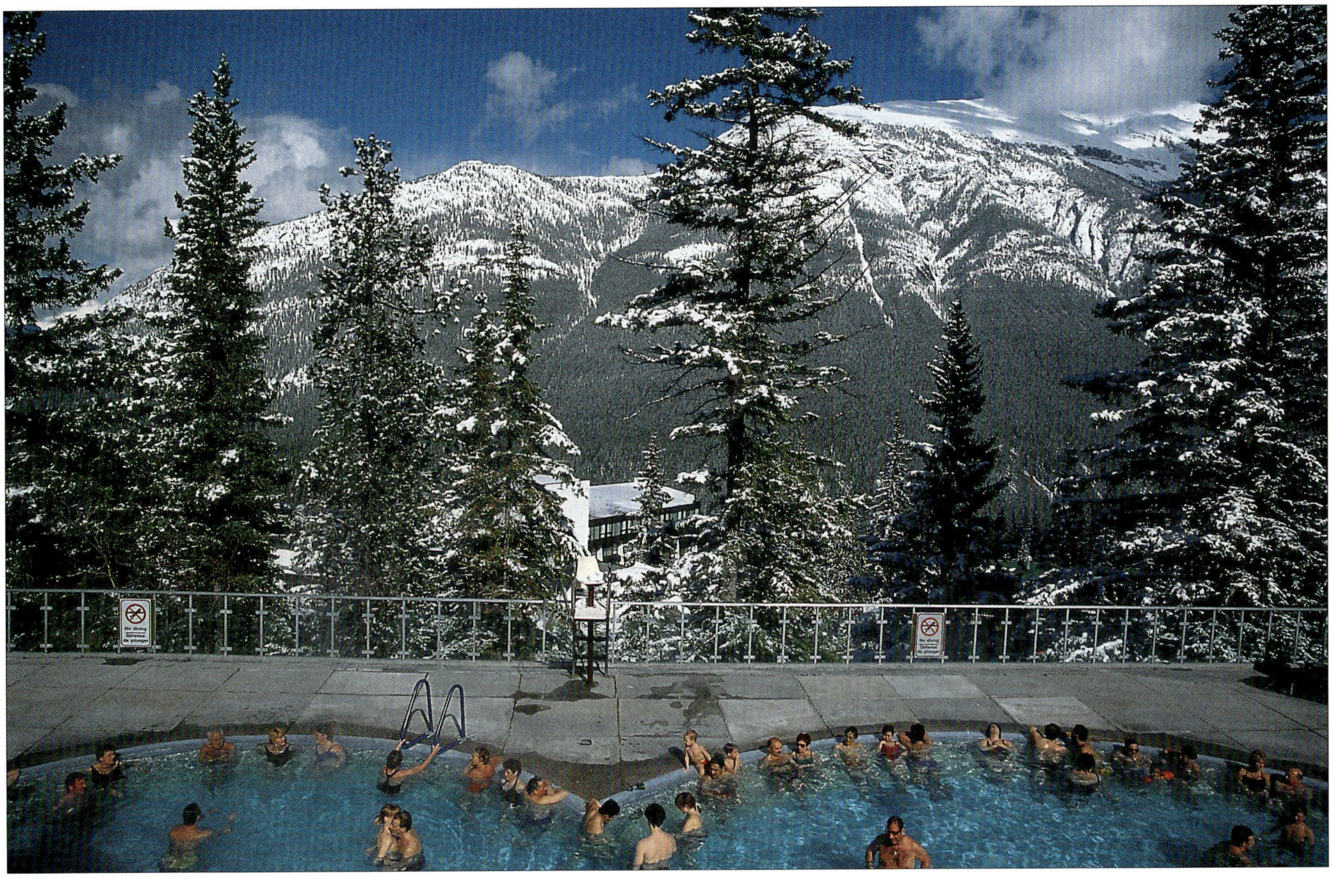

Top: A Mountain goat's white coat provides it with an excellent winter camouflage—as well as protection from the cold.

Middle left: During the winter it is common to see elk travelling in herds particularly around Banff townsite, the golf course and the Cave and Basin.

Middle right: The white-tailed ptarmigan, whose plummage changes colour with the seasons, is abundant in the Rockies.

Bottom: Although the wolf and coyote are similar in appearance to the untrained eye, the coyote, as seen here, is smaller, bolder, and more likely to be seen travelling through the valleys.

Top: Mule deer are frequently seen throughout the Banff and Lake Louise areas.

Middle left: Moose, tend to range high during winter, grazing on willows, aspens and poplars. An occasional moose can be spotted along the Bow Valley Parkway.

Middle right: Bighorn sheep are often seen licking salt from roadways or eating grasses along the Bow Valley Parkway west of Banff or near the Minnewanka Lake loop.

Bottom: Perched here on a ski pole, the Gray jay, also known as a whiskey jack or camp robber, is sure to brighten the darkest days of winter with its antics.

Ice climber Joe Josephson ascends a frozen waterfall—a vertical sheet of ice. This is a popular sport in the Banff/Lake Louise area, often lasting for five to six months. With ice axes in their hands and crampons fastened to their boots, ice climbers accomplish their feats by fastening metal anchors into the ice for safety.

Jo-Jo, as he is known to his friends, is an author and photographer, as well as one of the area's best-known ice climbers.

WINTER RECREATION

Young skaters enjoy ice-covered Two Jack Lake.

Snowshoeing through an aspen forest.

Snow is a key element in a Canadian Rockies winter. It starts falling high in the mountains in October and by mid-to-late November, many ski lifts are open and skis and snowboards are waxed and ready to go.

The snow falls slowly but constantly during the autumn months, making the sharp, jagged mountain peaks soften under a thick white layer of winter powder. Often, the valleys remain clear of snow for quite some time while the higher elevations continue to build an ever deepening base.

This is the time that ski areas wait for each year. For Sunshine Village, this natural snow base is the start of a very long season of 100% natural-based skiing and snowboarding. For Lake Louise and Banff Mount Norquay, this natural base is augmented by the latest in artificial snow-making equipment.

Once the ski season has commenced, Banff and Lake Louise begin their second life. The equipment shops replace their summer hiking gear with snowboards and skis. Bike rental stores become ski repair and ski rental outlets. Light summer parkas and tee shirts are supplanted with fleece and down-filled outerwear.

For those who are interested in equipment, there is a wide range of snowboards, downhill and cross-country skis, ice-climbing equipment

Two kids share a "moment" on a chair lift.

Sun tanning is an integral part of skiing.

and winter camping gear to choose from. Skiers and boarders from all over the world replenish their supplies or receive an expert tune-up in Banff before hitting the slopes.

Many top competitive events are held in the Banff/Lake Louise area. World Cup races as well as North American and Canadian Championships draw some of the world's best downhill, slalom and Super G competitors. Other events include aerial skiing, cross-country skiing, snowboarding and mixed races which combine snowshoeing with downhill and cross-country skiing.

Recreational skiers and snowboarders are provided with the best of all possible worlds. Novice runs and excellent beginner classes are a good starting point for new skiers. All the ski areas feature a huge selection of intermediate runs over a wide variety of slopes and terrains. For the expert skier and snowboarder, there are many challenging runs—including mogul fields, deep powder, tree-covered or vertical drop areas.

Best of all are the stunning, spectacular views of one of the world's most beautiful places. The top of the ski lifts provide what appears to the naked eye as an endless view of mountain peaks and a veritable frozen ocean. And on the route down, this grand vista changes with each twist and turn.

Winter in the Canadian Rockies. Perhaps this *is* heaven on earth.

Opposite: Here comes Santa Claus.
Opposite top, left and right: The powder flies on a blue-sky day.

Top: Two skiers appear to fly down a run at Sunshine Village. There are three major ski areas around Banff/Lake Louise.

Bottom: Upside down in a half pipe. Snowboarding is a major activity in the Canadian Rockies.

Opposite left and right: Moguls and powder—the best of both worlds.

Banff Mount Norquay

Top: Just ten minutes from the townsite, Banff Mount Norquay promises excitement for every level of skier. The renowned *Lone Pine* bump run thrills the experts, while the Cascade Chair (lower right) is perfect for the novice. Norquay's youth ski training program is one of Canada's finest.
Bottom: Mystic Ridge, which opened in 1990, features two quad chairs and long intermediate runs.

Opposite: Part of Banff Mount Norquay's Mystic Ridge.

Opposite inset: Three skiers on upper Excalibur Run get spectacular views of Norquay's base area as well as the Banff townsite and Mount Rundle.

SUNSHINE VILLAGE

Opposite: A three-mile gondola ride from the parking area to Sunshine Village ski area affords its passengers with a panoramic view of Mount Bourgeau.

Opposite inset: An 84-room inn graces the base area of Sunshine Village.

Top: The base at Sunshine lies below Goat's Eye Mountain which was opened for skiing in 1996.

Bottom left: High speed quad chairs lift skiers past views of Mount Assiniboine.

Bottom right: Moonlight adds punch to the already striking landscape of Sunshine Village.

One of the highest ski areas in Canada, Sunshine is known for its 750 centimetres (300 inches) of natural snow each year, which brings out the powder hounds as well as those who relish groomed trails. Sunshine boasts one of North America's longest seasons, with the resort open from November into late May.

On-hill accommodation makes Sunshine Village a perfect family resort destination. Day care and instructional programs are available for children, and many exciting events for the entire family take place throughout the season.

The ramparts of Castle Mountain tower at 3,041 metres (9,980 feet) above the turquoise waters of the Bow River.

LAKE LOUISE

Opposite: Lake Louise ski area rises above the Chateau Lake Louise. The ski area offers downhill runs above treeline as well as through the lower tree-covered slopes.
Top: Mount Lefroy (left) and Mount Victoria (centre), both over 3,300 metres (11,000 feet) form a majestic backdrop behind Lake Louise.
Bottom left: The recently reno-vated 511-room Chateau Lake Louise can accommodate just over 1,000 guests. The original chateau, built in 1890, was a log structure.
Bottom right: The annual Lake Louise loppet attracts hundreds of cross-country racers who help to raise money for charity.

Top: The back side of Lake Louise ski area, accessed by several lifts, presents skiers with one of the largest and most diverse collection of bowls and snow fields in the Rockies. This area is also the starting point for cross-country skiers wishing to tour the vast backcountry or to visit Skoki Lodge.

Opposite: Two skiers on Grizzly Ridge at Skiing Louise area appear to be skiing right next to the Chateau Lake Louise and the incredible glacier backdrop of Mount Victoria in this telephoto view. The scenery of Skiing Louise has been annually voted *No. 1* or *The Best in North America* by Snow Country magazine readers.

Bottom: Temple Lodge, at the base of the Larch expanse of Lake Louise ski area, is a lovely log building nestled between spectacular views and long ski runs. Spring skiers can work on their tans between runs, giving the large patio deck at the lodge its moniker, "Temple Beach."

Skiing Louise offers something for everyone: snowboarding, deep powder, wild jumps. World Cup events are often held at Lake Louise.

At the top of the page, Urs Walleser carves a tidy right turn on his snowboard. At the bottom, Banff resident Thomas Grandi, 1995 and 1996 National Giant Slalom Champion, hits the gate in another spectacular Grand Slalom effort.

accommodation at the lodge.

Top: In the summertime, Moraine Lake and the Valley of the Ten Peaks is one of Banff National Park's most popular destinations. This impressive winter view however, is attained only by cross-country skiing along a fourteen-kilometre trail starting from the Chateau Lake Louise access road.

Bottom: Jennifer Lee chops fire-wood to warm cross-country skiers visiting rustic Skoki Lodge. Located just over fourteen kilometres from Lake Louise, good skiers can travel in and out in one day. However, most prefer to stay overnight to enjoy the gourmet meals, pioneer atmosphere and camaraderie that have rewarded visitors for decades. Reservations are required for overnight

Top: Mount Temple 3543 metres (11,626 feet), is the third largest peak in Banff National Park and is thus a popular challenge for mountaineers. It is the highest peak in the Lake Louise region. This east face was first climbed in summer 1931, but was not climbed in winter until 1977, when local climber Tim Auger and his partner Uli Pfaelli reached the summit.

Bottom: The most spectacular winter drive in the Rockies is on the Icefields Parkway, or Highway 93 North. Historically called "The Wonder Trail," it is 230 kilometres of never-ending mountain peaks, glaciers, lakes, rivers and wildlife. The Icefields Parkway is a remote winter drive that is a must see but one that must also be respected. Its extreme beauty can be quickly tempered by sudden changes in weather and temperature. The road is frequently closed; please check with local authorities before setting out.

A Winter Portfolio

A wood-carved cowboy stands silhouetted against the
frosty panes of Skoki Lodge in Banff National Park.

– page 50 –
A small cluster of evergreens are a blaze of light above a
deeply shadowed ridge of winter snow.

– page 51 –
Rabbit tracks take a sharp turn on a powdery slope.

– page 52 –
The peak of Storm Mountain in Banff National Park.

– page 53 –
Snow blows across the face of Cascade Mountain near Banff.

– page 54-55 –
The Palliser Range provides a magnificent
backdrop for the Bow River.

– page 56 –
A mountain goat picks his way along a snowy ridge.